Through the Eyes Eyes Of a Man

BESIMBOLIC LESSONS

SIMEON HENDERSON

ISBN:1541207483
ISBN-13:9781541207486

BESIMBOLIC: being deeply rooted stimulates growth.
Quote by Simeon Henderson

BESIMBOLIC: The ability to envision a triumphant path through a web of chaos is simply the mindset of taking life's upsets and turning them into the force that drives your success. It is the ability to envision a triumphant path through a web of chaos. *"Through the Eyes of a Man"* is lined with episodes from my life where I take a candid look at those challenges, which should have slayed me, but were the bricks used to make me strong. Each lesson learned from my journey is a BESIMBOLIC LESSON.

"Through the Eyes of a Man" was written to reach those who may feel as I did; humiliated, mediocre, despondent, misjudged and empower them with tools that will ultimately allow them to refocus their perception of life making clear the idea that they are the author and finisher of their destiny. *"Through the Eyes of a Man"* was written to show others that no matter how deterring a situation seems, they have to believe that they are victorious and that, "They have the final say in their life"!

Simeon Henderson

CONTENTS

FOREWORD

You *know* Simeon. He is the guy that is so likable, fun, affectionate, outgoing and on…and on… and on. He gives you the impression that you've known him all your life. When you talk to him he puts you at ease and radiates a "feel good" vibe. Conversations with him flow easily. The laughter is genuine and robust. The zest for life is contagious. Being in his presence is uplifting. Simeon was a student in my classroom at Thomas Jefferson Elementary School in Chicago, IL. Even as a child there was a spark within him that turned heads and made people take notice of his many talents and potential.

During the time he served in law enforcement, he looked authoritative, yet approachable, in his police uniform. On TV he's a congenial host, and when performing, a convincing actor. He is a powerful motivational speaker and an enthusiastic influence on both children and adults alike. Did Simeon grow up with the proverbial "silver spoon in his mouth"? *"Just who is this guy?"* And that, is the million dollar question.

"Through the Eyes of a Man", *this* man, we travel back through his life escorted through episodes that gave him the vision he has today. Simeon makes us feel as though we are in a parallel version of the timelessly acclaimed novel, "A Christmas Carol" by Charles Dickens. Along with Simeon, we are transported back through times of hardship, fear, and devastation intertwined with times of wonderful surprises, enlightenment, and triumph - the ups and downs of what is typically called "life".

As we stand with him gazing at the vignettes so intimately and vividly detailed in this book, we are not left hanging. When each "ghost of…" returns us to present day reality, we have been enriched by a *Besimbolic* nuance. "A what?" you say. That's a new word.

After reading this treasure of a book, concise as a pearl in an oyster shell that is oh, so valuable, you'll discover how to *Besimbolic*, use it, and live it.

As you travel with Simeon looking through *his* eyes, the eyes of *this* man, "…be ye transformed by the renewing of your mind", Romans 12:2. Your third eye may emerge and allow you to reprocess your life in a different manner. To find out how all this happens, just keep turning the pages…happy reading!

Written by Lorea Farley, one of Simeon's elementary school teachers. Simeon, you are every teachers' dream come true!

Besimbolic!

ACKNOWLEDGMENTS

First, giving all honor to God who makes all things possible, I extend deepest gratitude to my wonderful wife Tammy Henderson and our beautiful children Vianey, Simeon II and Cj for your love and support through all the ups and downs. I know my journey can be tough on the family but I'm thankful for you hanging in there with me baby. Love you.

My siblings, the people who knew me best; my brother Jacob, Danyel and my sister Charra were always my best friends. Thanks! I can not forget my cousins who were just as close to me as my sister and brothers; Jamel, McKinley, Rosiland, Yvette (God rest her soul) Man, Rhonda, Jasmine, Daron, Marlon, Nikki, Nick. Thanks for your love. I'm so thankful that our parents raised us to share, love and appreciate each other.

My cousin/brother Reggie Robinson who has handled all of my public and electronically based affairs for the past 10 years.

Dwayne Bryant for helping me and showing me how to grow as a motivational speaker and mentor and giving me my first paid commencement speech. Just always encouraging me to go further.

To my God brother Johnny for always having my back, keeping it real with me and always paying for breakfast when I was broke.

Special thanks to Bruce Guthrie, Chris Adams, Darrin DeShaver, Dave Abrams, Papa, Joe DeCerbo, Mama Debbie. I cannot forget TJ and Beck, my Italian God parents for treating me like a son and helping me get through some of the toughest spots and college. Love you guys so much!

My partner Tony Whitfield who has mentored, supported and has been there with me on this journey by giving me advice, doing promo videos, scripts, insight and most importantly just being my brother. Our birthdays are on the same day September 9th. I won't put your year on here Tone. LOL!

To my sister, Lynne Parrott, for all the support and guidance on this journey of completing my book and just being a voice of reason and always having my back. Thank you for editing my book and making sure everything was on point. I love you all with all my heart.

Thanks to Camille Bradshaw for assisting with the editing process.

My friends growing up who motivated these memories like Tyree, Mike a.k.a. Nose, Terry, Steve, Drano, Nunu, Mary, Latrice, Mattie, Maria, Adnan, Vernie this was just to name a few. I must mention my brothers; Aubrey Lenard, Roger Washington, Tim Ervin and my best friends Ron Harris and Nate Glenn. I cannot forget to give a huge shout out to all my friends from Streamwood Class of '91.

Special thanks to Big O and Little Ociepka; my coaches. Thanks to Mr. Levitan, Mr. Barnett, Mrs. Ociepka, Mr. Miller, Miss Weaver, Ms. Lorea Farley, Miss Otto, Mr. Cole , Miss Colar, Miss Wells, Miss Williams, and the Special Ed staff at Jefferson Elementary for pushing me as a young person to greatness. Finally, my eighth-grade teacher/godfather, Mr. Harold Campbell for taking the role of my father when he wasn't there and his wife Lovie for allowing him that opportunity.

Enjoy the Read!

Through the Eyes Of a Man

Dedicated to the memory
of my Mom, Emma
and my Dad, Clem.

1
SLAYING YOUR GOLIATH

The Bible records an infamous story about a young man named David who fearlessly slayed a nine-foot giant Goliath to save his people. The story draws a portrait of a bully who taunted a nation for days and it wasn't until someone with enough courage and nothing else to lose tried what no one else had tried and successfully defeated that bully. Even though this story occurred around 1024 BC, it serves as a life-changing lesson with purpose and meaning for today's society.

The story of David and Goliath illustrated that even when presented with challenges that may seem to be larger than life, how you handle it will determine the outcome of your success. *Slaying your Goliath* means facing your issue and finding the solution.

Writing this book brought me full circle with many issues in my life. As a child and young adult, life presented many challenges. To look at me now one would never imagine the adversities I faced growing up. At an early age, I made the choice not to allow those adversities or "giants" to slay my purpose. I had the idea to look at life through the eyes of a young man who decided to stand up against all odds and slay giants one by one. The first Goliath I overcame was the giant of a bully.

As a child, school represented a place of pure torment, a mini version of hell. I remember it like it was yesterday. Sweat forms on my brow as I reflect on life as a kindergartener. Agonizing over the idea of going to school because of being terrorized by a bully was not the way to be introduced to the concept of a learning environment. It did not start immediately, but once the torture began, it was consistent.

Every morning, the teacher would call the class to the circle and each time my bully made their way next to me for the sole purpose of slapping my head and demanding that I "shut up". By recess, this person would have me too afraid to play and by the end of the day, all I wanted to do was run home to safety. The worst part about this daily perceived eminent threat to my life was that my abuser, the demon seed that had me afraid to blink, was a GIRL! Yes, I Simeon Henderson, was once bullied by a girl.

She was not just an ordinary girl. No, she was a GOLIATH GIRL compared to the other five and six year olds in the classroom. Standing three times my size in height and easily weighting in at more than double my body weight, she was the biggest girl in the primary department!

When I tell people about this horrific part of my elementary school journey they always asked me the same question, "What did your mother do?" What did my mother do? First, let us get this clear, even at five years old I understood the "Man Law" so I refused to tell my mother I was being bullied by a girl. "Man Law" stated that "boys are not supposed to be afraid of girls." I could not tell my father, the militant. I couldn't.

Embarrassment kept me from getting the help I needed so as long as I were quiet, she continued to slap me around. The shame of being transparent, even to my parents would not let me ask for help.

Besimbolic Lesson: Don't be afraid to speak up and ask for help when your problem seems overwhelming.

"You have not because you ask not" a familiar passage in the Bible, which my Grandma paraphrased as, "a closed mouth won't get fed." Speaking up for yourself will get you some results. Good or bad, either way, beats being silent to your own desires. Many people feel like what they are going through in life is too embarrassing to discuss with others. No one wants to feel like they cannot handle their own trials. Going to God and seeking help is the best remedy but many times, God will send you the help you need but because of your pride, you rather not reach out for it.

Speak up when you need help. You give permission to your issues to slap you around when you remain silent about them. Know that even the biggest hero needed an assistant. When things become overwhelming a brave individual, a person seeking to slay their Goliath will request assistance. I took matters into my own hands and learned another valuable lesson.

Besimbolic Lesson: *Every action has a reaction.*

Internalizing the bullying as a form of embarrassment, my reaction was to become what I was afraid of. Because of this girl bullying me, I became a bully. Hurt people who do not confront their pain usually hurt others. I justified my bullying to being terrorized and picked on and in my juvenile mind; it was ok to do the same thing to someone else.

I began to terrorize a boy that was smaller than I was. I believed that doing this gave me a sense of control. Goliath girl continued to taunt me during the day and after school, I would chase my prey from school all the way to the project building where he lived only to catch him and do to him what was being done to be, hit him in the head and slap him around. It got so bad that his mother came to the school to pick him up. I did not care if his mother was around, if his brother was around, if his sister were around I would still chase him and fight him every day.

This all came to a head the day my mother found out that I had been misrepresenting my upbringing. "We aren't raising you to be a bully." She repeated as she swung her leather belt on my five-year-old behind. Moreover, they were not, but because I "leaned unto my youthful understanding of how to handle life"; I was doing what I thought I was supposed to.

My father was appalled. He taught me to stand up for myself and to never hit girls. He also taught me that you give people permission to mistreat you. When he found out about my behavior after being bullied, he first made me apologize to the young man and then forced me to stand up to the bully. He told me that if she hit me, I was to immediately turn to her and let her know that I was not going to continue to let her push me around and that I would tell the teacher. If she did not stop, he and my mom would come to the school and speak with her parents.

That next day, I rehearsed all the way to school what I was going to say. "Leave me alone!" I'm not going to keep letting you hit me!" I was ready for her. As I approached the line for the kindergarteners to stand while waiting for the teacher I overheard the playground assistant telling another teacher that she was glad to see that family leave. She said all those kids did was terrorized the other kids.

The bell rang and the teacher marched the class in line and I noticed the giant was not with us. Entering the classroom, I placed my backpack in my cubby and went to sit in the circle when my teacher announced that "Giant Girl" would not be with us anymore. She had transferred to another school. The joy that rushed through my body made me leap. I apparently was not the only kid she had been terrorizing because it seemed that the entire class joined my jovial dance. The teacher, understanding our delight allowed us 30 seconds before she asked us to calm down and all come to the circle.

That day, I promised myself that I would never mistreat anyone. I made the choice to be the person who made others smile. I never wanted to cause anyone to become afraid of me because bullying others has a long-term effect on people. I understood that then. I wish for this to be a lesson. Take note of my struggle being bullied and realise that bullying does not have to control or change who you are.

Besimbolic Lesson: Don't be afraid to name and face your Giant.

You do not have to accept it or be afraid. Say something to a teacher, parent or friend. Do not give anyone control over you. This causes you to walk in fear and it hinders your progress. Being bullied turned me into something that I wasn't " A Bully" Why? Because hurting people, hurt other people. Another dynamic I had to consider was my part in being silent. Many abused people allow giants to overcome their lives staying silent because of fear. Even though I was being hurt I said nothing out of shame. This prolonged the issue.

Speak up when you encounter injustice. Silence is never ok. You can help to end the vicious cycle of bullying.

---

1 OUT OF EVERY 4 STUDENTS REPORTED BEING BULLIED DURING THE SCHOOL YEAR.

National Center for Educational Statistics, 2015

REFLECTIONS
"Slaying Your Giant"

What are some of the giants in your life that have held you back from your success?

_____
_____
_____
_____
_____
_____
_____
_____

What is your plan of attack to eliminate giants?

_____
_____
_____
_____
_____
_____
_____
_____

2
SURVIVING THE WILDERNESS

When a person refers to a wilderness experience, they are placing their situation in a position of disfavor. The dictionary defines a wilderness as a place that is "uncultivated, uninhabited, and inhospitable." A wilderness can also represent an abandoned area. Wilderness experiences are those in which nothing feels prosperous. These experiences are dry and barren. There is a sense of hopelessness in a wilderness experience. The Bible speaks of a wilderness and it equates it as a place where God sends revelation. Per the spiritual definition of a wilderness experience, the wilderness is the place where your life gets an identity shift.

Besimbolic Lesson: *Everyone at some point will experience a wilderness moment. You can survive it.*

I can, as an adult and as a Christian, fully understand that concept as my life did have a paradigm shift while I was in my wilderness. As a child, that frame of thinking may not be grasped. Experiences while in a wilderness can either make or break you. They can either push you to be a better person, hold you captive to the ills placed on you or make you a bitter person.

Childhood trauma and abuse affect many children nowadays as they travel through their own wilderness. As a mentor, I see firsthand the effects of a child who is experiencing some form of abuse. These children tend to scope out others to hurt or they may be withdrawn and depressed. Most children remain stuck in their own wilderness of depression and anger until they learn to cope but the coping tools they gather can be drawn from the wrong source.

Crime, dropping out of school and sexual promiscuity can become coping tools. Until someone recognizes the child's journey through the wilderness and intervenes or the child finds the way to cry out for help, they tend to slip deeper and deeper into an abyss of pain. That was part of my wilderness journey. My deliverance came because someone constantly prayed for me.

The English writer, Aldous Huxley who penned "The Doors of Perception" once said, *"Experience is not what happens to a man. It is what a man does with what happens to him."* Life lessons and experiences offer wisdom. You make the choice. What happened to me as a child placed me on the path which molded me into the man I am today. Sometimes I had to endure its ugly reality. The reality which said, "this is going to hurt." The hurt that overcame me when my dad left.

By the time I was in fifth grade my parents had separated and my mother had a new boyfriend. He never liked me and the feeling was mutual. I despised him, maybe because I blamed him for my parents separation or because he really was a mean person. The best part of them being together was the birth of my little sister.

The day my dad left still plays in my head like a rerun of a television drama. I remember running home one day to share my day with him only to find out that he wasn't there. Unlike kids are today, kids were not privy to adult information. We were raised to stay in a "child's place". When adults were talking, we were to leave the room or not be interruptive. So, I sat in my room wondering what happened to my dad. I waited up that night until my mother forced me to go to bed. The next day, he wasn't there during breakfast and when I came home after school he still had not returned. Later that night, I overheard my mother telling someone on the phone that he was at his mother's house and that she really did not care to discuss it.

I was devastated. My world seemed to stop and the questions consumed me. Why did he leave? Was he mad at me? Where was he? Was he coming back? I remember slamming the door to my bedroom and flopping into bed crying as my mind replayed the words my mom had just said, "Dad was gone." My anger was not at her saying that but more at the idea of him leaving without saying anything to me. Even as a child, I knew that they were having a hard time. I heard some arguing and some doors slamming but I always saw them together the next day. He could have at least told me he was leaving us.

His departure placed a heaviness on me that should never be experienced by a child. A present father impacts the shaping of a child's life. Parents are responsible for setting the culture they want their child nurtured in and a strong father helps mold their child into the person he or she is supposed to become. Sons develop role models and daughters find their first hero. The absence of my father at such an early age made me begin to look for other role models.

It makes a huge difference when a young man and a young woman have their father present in their life. Having a father present and attentive is crucial in the development of our next generation it has been proven that Fathers represent security. Studies show that a child who lives in a household without their father is at a higher risk for social detriment, dropping out of school and participating in criminal activities. They are also at a higher risk of being victims of physical and sexual abuse at the hands of men brought into the home by their mothers.

If you are a Dad, mark your place in this book and take time to remind your child that you are always there for them. Solidify that bond daily before anger becomes the giant that overtakes your child's life.

A CNN report noted that in 2013, as many as 72% of African American children are raised in a single parent household. Men, fathers, we must stop dropping the ball on our children. They depend on us. They thrive from having us in their lives. I know my life changed early on as I was faced to live it without my dad at home.

For me, that all too real giant was not a simple one to slay and it left me feeling as a child depressed at times. Thinking back to that time I know that I was a child having a wilderness experience.

Grandma Henderson's home was right around the corner from our apartment so although he wasn't coming home he was within walking distance. One day I decided to visit him in search of my unanswered question – why was he not looking for me?

I got dressed, made sure that my chores were done and that my hair was combed. My mother had this thing about making sure that we kept our hair combed. It was a true reflection of her as she was always well groomed. When she got home, I asked permission to visit Grandma Henderson with the excuse that she had the best snacks and I missed her.

I wanted to see my father but couldn't tell her that I had overheard her conversation. She agreed but said that I had to be in the house before the street lights came on.

Excited, I ran to Grandma Henderson's house only to be met with further disappointment-he was not there that day. She was glad to see me and like most Grandmas, she fed me and showered me with hugs. Sending me off with a pocket full of candy, she hugged me and said, "I will let your Dad know you were looking for him. I never discussed him with her but she knew why I was visiting. She loved me and knew that I enjoyed visiting her but she also knew I missed my dad.

Visits to Grandma Henderson became a routine, as I was desperate to see my Dad. Every visit was full of kid friendly treats and a whole lot of love. She always had a word of encouragement, a joke and my favorite ice cream. I can still hear her saying to me, "Little Simmy, be good" as I walked from her house to mine at the end of my visit. Several times, I could catch him leaving the house or I would be leaving when he was arriving. The encounters were awkward; I became uneasy about questioning his decision to leave and instead cherished seeing him.

I had one Uncle who balanced me and filled the void my dad left, Uncle T. Uncle T kept me laughing. He and Aunt Carolyn were a joy to be around. My mother would tell me that I like being over Uncle T's house and Grandma Henderson's more than I like being at home. July 4th was my favorite holiday to visit Uncle T. He would buy a box of fireworks that was taller than me and he shared it with the neighborhood. I remember eating barbecue, listening to music, laughing, playing and setting off fireworks all night long. Growing up with Uncle T, I learned to adapt and be content. He was my "ram in the bush". Having Uncle T saved me in more ways than one. His support and encouragement gave me the courage to speak up about being abused.

I did not tell my mother or my uncles about the abusiveness of my stepfather and I wish now that I had. Every time I think back on the pain that he caused me, I am brought back to a place that I once hated. His rage only took place when he was left alone with me. He would just slap me or punch me for no reason. Along with the physical abuse came the verbal abuse. He would tell me, "you ain't never going to be anything and I hate you!" His insults always devalued my intelligence and potential. His words hurt me to the core, so much so I in turn began detesting my life.

I was constantly in a state of questioning-why it happened to me? What had I done to deserve being treated so badly? Why did he hate me so much? I mean it was terrible. It started with verbal abuse. He made it his daily task to remind me that I was "dumb" and "stupid" and that "I would grow up to be an idiot hooked on drugs." His words stung only because I hated him and could do nothing about returning that feeling to him. My family was free of abuse until he came in. I just wanted him gone.

I remember how bad I struggled with math. I could not seem to understand the formulas. He bragged about being great at it so one day my Mom asked him to help me with my math homework. While she was at home, everything was fine. He played the role of a dutiful, caring tutor. He patiently asked me questions and even coached me into ways to remember math strategies. Mom, thinking all was well gave me a kiss and left to run errands. That was when hes personified into the "Real McCoy". Winking his eye at me when as she closed the door, I knew something was up. As soon as he came back to the table to finish helping me, the insults began. I became all kinds of "dumb MFs, and stupid SOBs". Every time I got a problem wrong, he would hit me and flare insults at me. The first answer was incorrect and as promised, he slapped me. The next few problems were also incorrect and he repeated the punishment. The fear of being beaten along with the knowledge of my fight with understanding the math made it difficult for me to think.

"Come on boy, I don't have all day to be dealing with your stupid behind" is what he blurted out as he paced the floor pounded his fist into his hand. I cried out, "I'm trying". Before I knew it, he began to punch me in the face. He hit me so many times until blood began to run from my nose as if someone had opened a tap. When I asked to go to the bathroom to stop the bleeding, he told me to just sit there saying he did not care if I bled to death. I did not move from that spot. Hearing my mother returning, he handed me a wet paper towel to clean up my face and gave me enough of the answers to look as if he were really helping me. I was too afraid to tell my mother. I just wanted to forget it even happened. Therefore, I went to bed and cried until I fell asleep.

On another occasion, he chased me out of the kitchen, onto the porch and kicked me in my back causing me to fall down a flight of stairs simply because I drank a glass of his grape juice. Lying at the bottom of the flight on my face in tears, I heard him at the top of that flight. His laughter and abusive words continued. Again, fear kept me from telling my mother.

One day, I accompanied him and his friend on an outing. His actions were unfamiliar-his kindness made me nervous but it was better than having him beating on me so I played along with it. He promised me fast food when he was done handling business with his friend, I was told to sit at the window at this apartment building in a location that I was not familiar with. He told me to be his lookout. Therefore, for this fast food, I sat at the window of an empty apartment and did what he told me which was to look out the window and to call him if I saw a police. I had no idea why he told me that but my young mind was on the food payout.

Hunger hit me about two hours into this lookout gig so I walked to the kitchen where he and his friend were to remind him about the promised burger and fries. As I entered the kitchen, I saw the two men standing next to the counter wearing mask, white gloves and what look like a scale with a bunch of white powder on it. I walked into what I now know was them packaging drugs. Trying to act as if I did not see the apparent elephant in the room, I looked straight at him and told him I was hungry. Running towards me he knocked me to the floor and screamed, "I told you not to move from that window and tell me if you saw the police."

The rage in his voice, the piercing look in his eyes and his puffed body posture scared me. I wet my pants. Hitting me again, this time in the face, he and his friend laughed and teased me for being wet. He made me go back to the window and continue to wait for him, smelly pants and all. We were there another hour and I stood wet and hungry. This was a very tough time in my life especially since I felt I could not tell anyone. I knew that my uncles would have killed him and I did not want them getting into any trouble. So, I endured the abuse.

Some days he would just slap me and call me names. Other times I was his human punching bag. Rarely would we be alone and he not put his hands on me. It got to the point where I hated being at home or anywhere alone with him.

No child should ever have to experience abuse. The bad thing about this is that I told myself that when I got old enough and strong enough that I was going to kill him because I was that mad at what he did to me. If it wasn't for God, my mother and my faith, I honestly think that I would've tried to kill him.

God had to have heard my prayers one day and declared that enough was enough. This day my stepfather made the mistake of slapping me and not realizing that my Uncle T saw him.

"Hey, what the hell", was what I heard from across the living room. My stepfather had followed me in the room telling me how stupid I looked when he asked me something and I did not respond. His habit instructed him to slap me after he insulted me. This time he and his habit were about to get checked.

The look on my Uncle's face clued me that he did not agree with what he had witnessed. Walking over towards him, my uncle grabbed him by his neck and walked him over to the window saying to him that if he ever touched me again he would be tossing him out of that window. My uncle told my mother and well I must say that was the last time my stepfather ever put his hands on me.

When my mother found out what had been going on she was torn. Hugging me she cried and apologized for allowing him into our life. She reminded me how much she loved me, leaned over and kissed me on the forehead, stood straight, wiped her eyes and went into beast mode. The next thing I knew she was packing his things and telling him he had to go.

The funny thing about the whole situation is that after twenty plus years, the few times I saw him he acted like

none of that ever happened. Speaking to me as if he was
the dutiful, fun stepdad he told himself he was he would
extend his arms to hug me or joke with me like we were
buddies. Although I hated what he did to me as a child, I
made up my mind to forgive him. Having the talk with
him one day about my life when he was in it gave me an
idea to his state of mind. He truly had no thought to what
his abuse was doing to me. My releasing him by telling
him I forgave him left a look on his face that was
priceless. I confessed to him my desire as a kid to kill
him when I got older but that I was so much bigger than
that and I made the choice to let it go.

Even though, he wanted me to believe that he was
oblivious to his actions, I needed him to hear directly
from me how I was affected but because of God and my
mother I could genuinely begin the process of
forgiveness and be a bigger man.

It was part of my testimony as to how to overcome
the bad things in our lives. I later found out and saw the
physical abuse he placed on his own son and I knew he

had no desire to change. Recognizing that hurt people, hurt people, I understand that this was just who he was. He was probably one of those wilderness walkers who never found a path out. I prayed for him and asked God to show me how to totally forgive him so that I could truly move on.

Forgiveness is powerful! Being able to let things go is a sign of growth. It is not easy to do. For years, I hated him. For years, I wanted him dead. I have made the choice today to be cordial to him but I will not allow him in my circle because although I have forgiven him, I will not forget it. Yet, I refuse to let that stop me. I won't be held in bondage to what life dealt me.

We can't let our past hurts hold us captive, meaning that if we don't let things go and move forward they will hold us back and keep us from walking towards our destiny. I was abused, and yes it was a terrible experience for any child to have to go through, but at the end of the day God spared my life so I could encourage and inspire others. Please know that no matter what, if you stay faithful and focused you will overcome and help someone else.

Be encouraged to make a difference because your story matters. I must thank God for the people he surrounded me with while in my wilderness. These individuals, mostly family, helped rejuvenate me.

"WE CAN'T LET OUR PAST
HURTS HOLD US CAPTIVE,
MEANING THAT IF WE DON'T
LET THINGS GO AND MOVE
FORWARD THEY WILL HOLD US
BACK AND KEEP US FROM
WALKING IN OUR DESTINY."

REFLECTIONS
"Surviving the Wilderness"

What are some of your wilderness experiences?

_____
_____
_____
_____
_____
_____
_____
_____

What did you take away from it?

_____
_____
_____
_____
_____
_____
_____

3
FACING CONSEQUENCES

Growing up angry at my father for leaving and not caring enough about my step father to listen or learn anything from him, I basically had to become a man by trial and error. Many times, I would find myself in trouble and working hard to get out of it, I would use every tactic I could. Most of the times, had I just confessed and taken my punishment, things would have been easier for me.

Besimbolic Lesson: *Learn to face your consequences and become stress free.*

Life will give you times where you need to make the decision that may not feel right. If that decision is based on holding on to your integrity, that is the one you want to make. There is this saying that God will send you a ram in the bush. That is true, but don't get used to looking for that ram. I had to learn that lesson the hard way.

Grandma Jackson, my mother's Mom, lived on the second floor of our building and we lived on the third. I say our building because it was owned by my grandfather, Reverend Johnny Jackson and ran like a "family building". Where Grandma Henderson fed me, Grandma Jackson kept me safe, safe from the wrath of my mother. I remember it like it was yesterday and will always thank God for the presence of Grandma Jackson.

The set up went like this. I would do something that would get me into trouble with my mother who would then stomp into the living room declaring war on my behind. At that point, I would do what I had to distract her while pleading for one more chance. It would begin with an overdramatic flop to the floor then move to the panic-stricken begging for my life, kicking and scream until I heard my Grandma yelling for my mother to stop whipping me. Mom, knowing that I was trying out for an Oscar, would ignore the first command from Lieutenant Grandma Jackson and just like clockwork Grandma Jackson would come in busting through the door and announce with her voice of authority,

"Emma stop! You killing that boy".

At that point Grandma Jackson would get between my mother and I grabbing me by my hand, removing me from the battlefield and charting me off to safer grounds, like her apartment. You know I put on the real act then. Huffing and puffing, face full of tears, the entire show. Now, I do know that I was way too old to be acting out like that but, I knew it would draw the response I wanted.

Once I got bold enough to glance back at my mother and smiled as Grandma Jackson declared the war over. Walking me out of the door Grandma Jackson thought the mascaraed was over but I knew it wasn't as I could see the "just wait" smirk come across her face. I soon learned that, my Mom, the original playwright in my life, she was writing another scene to this script and it wasn't looking good for me. She was always in control of this production.

That day came sooner than later for me. One day, I was playing basketball in the closet, (something my Mom had told me numerous times not to do) and broke the rail in the closet. Not aware that my Mom was downstairs and heard all the commotion, I tried unsuccessfully to quickly repair the damage. As I struggled to put the railing back on the wall, my Mom rushed into my room. "Boy were you playing in that closet?" She asked and for some dumbfounded reason I answered her, "No".

Noticing my closet in disarray, the railing in my hand and the basketball on the floor she immediately went into what I called "beast mode". See my mother was the sweetest person you ever knew until you lied to her. Once that happened, Beauty turned in to the Beast. Without question, she pulled her belt from somewhere (to this day I don't know where) and begin to slay my back side while speaking in beast language. To me it sounded like a slow-motion recording.

"You going to stand there and tell me that lie?" Every word bore what seemed like five lashes. I found my way to the threshold of my bedroom and flopped slamming my hands against the floor clueing my Grandma to the killing spree Mom was on.

"HA, HA, HA, HA". This piercing sound of torture exploded from my Mom's delicate frame. I had to turn to see if indeed my Mom was being transformed. She was enjoying this way too much and I was now scared.

"Grandma!" I yelled as I continued to beat an SOS message on the floor. Mom paused and inhaled. The room got quiet. It reminded me of a scene from the movie "Twister" when the eye of the storm passed. I turned again to assure that Mom was still Mom and she softly replied, "You can kick and scream all you want", she said with a smile on her face, "your grandma is not home." She chuckled as she gathered the belt in both hands, popped it and said a bit louder, "She's not at home."

That was the day I was forced to man up and face my consequences. The scenario was the same, I got in trouble and my mom took out that belt which was my clue to hit the floor and go into action kicking and screaming but this time, she knew she had the upper hand on me so she joined me in the performance. When she was finished, she told me that it would be so much easier for me to just tell the truth. If you are going to be man enough to disobey, be man enough to admit it and take what comes with your actions.

Besimbolic Lesson: *Man up when you mess up!*

I learned early in life that there is a price to pay for everything you do. That saying, "What's done in the dark will come to the light" is so true. You might be sliding through life thinking that your mess will never stink but I am here to warn you that it will catch up with you. It's easier to "man up" and confess than to continue to run and cover. Take responsibility for your part in any wrong doing and rectify it. Fix it!

This story of a young man running from punishment may seem a simple one but it is an example of how the wrong behavior patterns are set, change usually must come by force. The difficulty in rectifying wrong doings in the past, then lies in ones' willingness to be better.

People have been known to say that, "The past is the past and there is no reason to keep reliving it." But for many of them, if they had the power to change their past, they would. Deep inside people want right things to be done and injustices to be corrected. The fear of facing consequences usually becomes the draw back to correction. For me, it was the idea of receiving the wrath of my mother. Whatever the reason, live up to your role in it, honestly seek forgiveness and make every effort to not repeat your actions because there is truth in the one saying, "what's done in the dark will come to the light."

For every action, there is a reaction. This is a common fact. Never believe that what you do, intentionally or inadvertently means nothing. Like a boomerang, what you throw out comes back. Owning up to your boomerang brings a sense of integrity to you and allows for growth. "Man up!"

CONCEPTS MY MOTHER
INSTILLED IN ME AS A CHILD
REMAINED STAPLES ON HOW TO
WALK THROUGH LIFE.
"BE TRUTHFUL"
"MAN UP"
AND
"FACE YOUR CONSEQUENCES."

REFLECTIONS
"Facing Consequences"

Discuss a time in your life when facing your consequence forced growth.

_____
_____
_____
_____
_____
_____
_____
_____

How do you handle "man ups"?

_____
_____
_____
_____
_____
_____
_____
_____

4
WALKING ON WATER

My references to biblical stories come from my personal experiences of faith. Principles I developed from the premise of these stories are constant motivators in my life. I know that without the presence of God in my life and the level of faith I have achieved, I would be nothing. I learned that I must walk by faith. This chapter speaks to the ability to walk by faith and not by sight.

A famous passage in the Bible is used by many clergy, pastors, ministers and priest. It is the one where Jesus calls Peter out to "walk on water". This passage is used mainly as a focus on trusting God and having Faith regardless of what the visible circumstance is around you. Nature tells us that humans lack the capacity to physically walk on water. Gravity and added weight make that task a bit difficult.

History tells us that Leonardo da Vinci wanted to

walk on water so in the 15th century he invented a pair of pontoon-like shoes to fulfill that feat. Inspired by DaVinci's quest, Remy Bricka, a French Entertainer used a pair of floating skies to walk across the Atlantic in 1988. Although there have been many attempts at doing what God instructed Peter to do, it is almost next to impossible.

There is a force that is needed that will pull the body in the direction parallel to the water's surface. Common understanding of gravity, which is the force that pulls objects down towards the earth, reminds us that it is physically impossible for mankind to walk on water without assistance. Peter, a fisherman, clearly had that concept but, he trusted God and God told him to do it.

As the story goes, it wasn't until reality grabbed Peter during his walk of faith that he realized he was going against a force that wanted him to remain incapable of doing what God told him. It was at that point that Peter lost faith in his ability and began to sink. Peter allowed the issue of his current state to determine the outcome of his future based on either what was said to him in the past or his knowledge of that impossibility. Either way, he failed the challenge.

I equate "walking on water" to what it feels like to attempt the impossible. It is like fighting whatever is in you which tells you that it can't happen with that still small voice which says you can. Having faith in yourself against all odds is equivalent to walking on water.

When on a walk of faith, one needs to remind themselves of their past triumphs. Others will remind you of your failures, you can believe that. Faith is about starting with a mustard seed, watering it and watching it grow. Everyone has one thing they can say worked for their good. Remind yourself of that time. I believe had Peter taken the time to remember who Jesus was, what miracles he had done, and even the mere fact that Jesus was walking on the same water he told Peter to walk on, Peter would have kept his eye on the prize and continued his journey. He would have kept his focus on Christ.

There are several things from my past I have chosen to cherish. These things I use the same way that God used the thorn in Paul's side; to keep me humble. I always knew that God had purpose for me but I should stay focused and not allow distractions to distort my vision. I knew as a child that I was different. I always wanted to see the glass as half full and I always wanted others around me to be happy. I did not understand it as being my purpose as a motivator, I just knew it felt like I was born to encourage and make others smile.

This thorn indeed humbled and kept me focused. Where life experiences could have that stunned my personal, spiritual and emotional growth this thorn pushed me to greatness. You see, in grammar school I was labeled "LD" or to be politically correct "Learning Disabled". That notice became a thorn in my side and this letter gave me the strength to keep moving regardless.

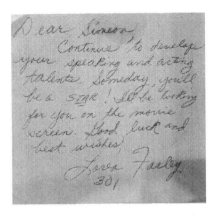

The irony behind this letter is that it was given to me after I was told by another teacher that I wasn't smart enough because I couldn't read and I wasn't a good speller. This teacher informed me that I would not ever be good at math, and that I probably wouldn't be too successful in life because I lacked the ability to obtain a good education.

Besimbolic Lesson: Your words carry power.

Now I don't know about you but that's some pretty messed up stuff to tell a10-year-old kid. I was in the fifth grade when the label "LD" was added to my academic bio and I will never forget how it made me so mad. At an early age, I said that I would be able to do whatever I put my mind to. I became determined to shake the stigma of being labeled anything that embarrassed me. I went out and asked for help on my own.

I asked a few teachers to help me after school with my reading and on days that they couldn't my Uncle Bay Bay took out time to read with me. My mother began to spend more time with me going over my homework and when no one was available, I pressed and worked harder on my own. I wasn't going to let that one teacher tell me what I could or couldn't do.

One motivation for the defeat of being titled "LD" was the love I had for basketball and my desire to be on the team. For anyone to be on the team, their grades had to be acceptable. Because of my noted "disability", there were exceptions that could have been put in place for the coach to bring me on to the team, but I did not want to be brought in on a curve. I was not going to be considered a "dumb jock" so I worked extra hard to overcome my deficiency.

The coach saw something in me and I could play on the team. He knew he had made the right decision when by the end of the sixth-grade I was one of the top basketball players in the school. My motivation to drop that "LD" label was fueled by the desire to wear the label of "MVP".

Besimbolic Lesson: *Do what makes you happy and make that your purpose.*

I fell in love with basketball. I started playing when I was eight years old. I would always go to the neighborhood court and watch my Uncle Joe and my Uncle Bay Bay play ball with their friends. There were a lot of things in my neighborhood on the west side of Chicago that could stop you from being successful if you let it.

Growing up on the near west side of Chicago in the neighborhood called the *Village* was where I obtained knowledge of the streets and the game of basketball. In my neighborhood, there wasn't much to choose from. We had one playground and one main basketball court. The little kids played in the playground and the big kids played basketball.

The basketball court sat in the middle of an open space surrounded by five project buildings. The main building was where the local gang, "Death Valley Gangsters" hung out so it was not foreign to hear gunshots or see drug paraphilia on the ground while playing basketball. Regardless of this, kids still wanted to play basketball.

I was eager to be a part of the street ball team my older cousin ran so I begin to hang with them showing them my skills. They saw the raw talent and told me that if I followed the rules they would let me play one day. I did everything they asked so my cousin Melvin decided to put me on the team telling the other guys that I was a risk taker and I knew the game. Having my cousin run the team has its advantages.

Hanging with the older guys gave me a huge boost of confidence. They weren't that much older than me but they fell in the divide line of playing in the playground and shooting hoops on the court. Uncle Joe and the other guys were around thirteen years old and I was only eight, so they made me their ball boy.

Watching the guys play, I was amazed at how good they were and I wanted to be just like them. My Uncle Joe and his friends grew up playing in the Medill gym, which was ran by my cousin Melvin Gun. We called him "Gun" for short. He was the no nonsense one out of the group. With the priority of empowering the neighborhood boys into becoming great men, Gun enforced morals and instilled a sense of value towards education. Uncle Bay Bay was fast and could handle the ball while Uncle Joe's tall, slim stature gave him the jump advantage. Each one had qualities, which I admired and worked hard to perfect.

I remember my first game we played in a tournament at Crane High school. It was so funny. I was the smallest guy on the court and everybody kept commenting on how enormous my uniform looked on me. At the time my mother was pursing her Associates Degree in nursing at Malcolm X College which was right around the corner from Crane so she came out to support the team.

The game started just as my mom arrived. Entering the building on the opposite side of the court, she looked across the court, saw me sitting on the bench and she ran across the court while the game was in session screaming, "There goes my baby!" My cousin Melvin Gun screamed back at her from across the court, "Emma girl get off the court!" All I could do was put my head down and laugh. That was my mom and she loved her babies. I don't know if I were more excited about being an eight-year-old kid playing my first basketball game with teenagers or having my mother's embarrassing support. By the end of the season, we won and walked away with the trophy. I still smile when I walk past my mantle and see that trophy and my Master's

Degree as they both stand as a reminder that when you believe in yourself, walking on water is possible.

---

*PETER ALLOWED THE ISSUE OF HIS
CURRENT STATE TO DETERMINE THE
OUTCOME OF HIS FUTURE BASED ON
EITHER WHAT WAS SAID TO HIM IN
THE PAST OR HIS KNOWLEDGE OF
THAT IMPOSSIBILITY.*

REFLECTIONS
"Walking on Water"

Name a time when you stepped out on faith.

_____
_____
_____
_____
_____
_____
_____
_____

What was the outcome?

_____
_____
_____
_____
_____
_____
_____
_____

4
BUILDING YOUR ARK

An Ark symbolizes something that affords protection and safety. Noah built an ark after God told him there would be rain. No one had seen rain before and they laughed at him when they saw him building a boat for something he did not need. Noah continued to build because he believed God and did not care what others thought.

Noah built his Ark away from others, especially those who did not believe in what he was doing, as he was protecting the destiny God presented to him. Noah was surrounded with supportive people. Building the Ark, Noah learned that he had to be patient and create a tenacity for getting the job done, regardless of the circumstances. Noah designed the Ark exactly the way God told him; he learned he had to follow the plan. And by the way, Noah was a drunk. He was somebody that people took little stock in. He was labeled by others and placed in the "will not succeed" section. Once Noah attached himself to the plan of destiny God gave him, none of those prior dynamics meant anything to him. He was creating a future for himself, his family and those who were to come after him.

BESIMBOLIC LESSON: *An effective teacher serves as an ark builder for children.*

Back in my day, teachers really seemed to take on the role of a parent at school and they received that kind of respect. When a person shows a child that they are vested in their education, the child thrives. Not taking anything away from teachers today but, let's face it, times are vastly different. Nowadays, everything is so political, you can't correct students without the fear of losing your job or even having a student possibly try and fight the teacher. From the level of respect for your elders to the demand on obtaining a quality education, life is viewed out of foggier glasses nowadays. The immediate delivery of education has changed a bit but, there are still many teachers who dedicate themselves to inspiring students. These individuals make a difference in the lives of their students.

Looking back, I had a few inspiring teachers in my path. Mr. Campbell and my grammar school basketball coach Mr. Ociepka, and made huge impacts in my life which in turn became their way of helping me build my ark.

My Dad was in and out of my life by the time I was in the sixth grade and on one occasion, Mr. Campbell had the opportunity to meet him. Instead of being a source of discouragement and speaking ill of my father, Mr. Campbell complimented him telling me that my dad was the best parent he ever had simply because he would check on me all the time. He said my Dad was a sharp dresser and could tell he was a man of pride. I had so much respect for Mr. Campbell as he saw the importance of building my father's image in my eyes than destroying it. Mr. Campbell quickly became my idol. Jokingly, I referred to him as "Mr. Campbell Soup" and I told him I was going to play basketball like he did, become a teacher like he was, and join Phi Beta Sigma fraternity like he did. By the way, all those things, I accomplished.

Mr. Campbell was a special mentor in my life along with Coach Ociepka who spent more time with us as a team than any other coach I knew. "Lil O" as he was known, would take the team members home, feed us, make sure we were doing good in school and always insisted that we be respectable young men. Lil O exposed us to different neighborhoods outside of what we were accustomed too and told us that we were valuable young men.

I think about the impact that they had on our lives to this day and I'm so thankful. These are the teachers that made a huge difference in my life at an early age they helped me to see that I did not have to let someone's opinion of me become my reality.

By the time, I got to eighth grade I was one of the top basketball players in the State of Illinois. Scoring fifty six points in one game caused me to be scouted by almost every high school in the city, but I had my hopes on being called to the team at Providence St. Mel High School.

Now as I went through my eighth-grade year I kept my grades up although I still had to go to a special class for reading and math I never let that stop me from working hard to be the best I could be. I was playing basketball our team was winning and we finished the season with a record of 72 and 10. Lil O had us play 82 games and we loved every minute of it.

BESIMBOLIC LESSON: *Friends are in your life for a reason, a season or a lifetime. Know the purpose of your friend.*

The best teammate I had back then happened to also be my best friend, Lamont Anderson. When we played basketball together people would refer to him as Magic Johnson and me Michael Jordan. He would pass the ball and I would score. Together we were a powerful duo. We hung out at his house and did everything together. Our moms were best friends and were always together so that gave us time to perfect our team building skills.

Lamont was part of my ark building crew. His ability, as my peer to believe in me was pivotal to my growth.

Part of building an ark is to surround yourself with people who are like-minded, people who will work with you, people who want the best for you. In life, Lamont was always there for me. His recent passing hurt but I know that even in heaven, he is expecting only the best in his friend. I thank God for having a friend like that.

When it was time to reach out to high schools, I pursued the only one I ever dreamed of attending, Providence St. Mel. Providence St. Mel was where my Uncle Joe Jackson went and I felt it drawn to be there. Uncle Joe was a legend at Providence St. Mel taking the basketball team into and winning a state championship. I remember attending all the basketball games and saying to myself that would be me one day. I told my mother of my choice of high schools and her first concern was the tuition. Providence St. Mel was an academically, prominent school with a highly successful basketball team that came with steep tuition

The dichotomy of feelings which took over me when I received the letter of acceptance into Providence St. Mel was all too real as on one hand I was thrilled to learn that I had been offered a partial basketball scholarship but worried about how my Mother was going to meet the remainder of $100 a month for my tuition. Mom prayed and told me not to worry.

I remember thinking about how far I had come. To even be accepted into a school, which offered as much as Providence St. Mel did, was an honor. I was a kid with an "LD" label and no money but I also was a kid who had conquered giants and experienced wilderness journeys. I was going to trust that God was making a way for my tuition to be paid.

My Uncle Bay Bay, the uncle who took me under his wings years before and taught me the game of street ball, found out that I was accepted into Providence St. Mel under a basketball scholarship and was as thrilled as I was. Uncle Bay Bay became a noted ark builder when he took on the responsibility of paying the monthly balance of my tuition telling my mother that I was going to get the best education I could if he had anything to do with it. My family was so proud of me and for once I was extremely proud of myself.

During eight grade my relationship with my Dad began to flourish. Having him apologize for not being in my life as much was huge for me. He told me that he wanted to make that up to me and promised to meet with me at school every day and take me to the Patio, a neighborhood restaurant, for our favorite meal; hot dogs and fries. Every day he came, he was dressed to kill. His suave demeanor and sharp suits became his signature for people around the neighborhood. I loved being with my dad and to me, life was taking a turn for the better, or at least it was until the day my dad was robbed.

I guess the thugs in the neighborhood perceived my dad's fashion statement for a bank statement when they decided not only to rob him at gunpoint but to shoot him in the head.

When I got the news, I was devastated. My mom took my brother Jacob and I to the hospital and we waited there until we could see him. I remember trying to hold back tears as the fear of losing my dad was all I could think about. Walking into the hospital room, seeing my dad attached to machines and hearing beeping sounds enhanced my fears. I could see from the entrance of the room, the blood on the bandage which was wrapped around him head and I froze. Mom walked me closer to my dad as he noticed we were in the room.

The closer I got to his bed, the harder I cried. My dad, my tower of strength laid with a bullet hole in his head. This was not supposed to be like this. My dad would not hurt anyone. I continued to cry as my dad slowly slide his hand from the side of the bed and grabbed mine. "Simmy", he whispered. Stop crying. I'm going to be all right." The sound of his voice, even in a whisper gave me hope.

Even though it was difficult seeing him lying there fighting for his life in pain I knew that I had to do as he asked and hold back the tears. If he could be selfless being more concerned with how I was feeling, I had to put away my fears and walk this journey with him. It took a while but my dad made a full recovery and promised me to make it to my eighth-grade graduation. I was excited because Mr. Campbell chose me to deliver a speech and this would be my first time speaking in front of a large audience.

Now you must remember I was in the LD class and I was told that I probably wasn't going to make it, but here I stood ready to graduate and ready to go to high school. I stood ready to prove to the world that I was not a dumb jock, that I could be successful in anything I put my mind to. When it came time for me to give my speech, I was terrified. The words of advice that my Dad gave me that morning pushed themselves to the front of my mind. He said, "Simmy, when you walk up to the podium take a deep breath look at the people, smile, take another deep breath and read your speech. When it's over smile and say thank you". Those words helped take away my fear and started to mold me into the man that I would become.

Whenever I prepare to go on stage, I do exactly what my Dad told me. Words of wisdom never age.

As this chapter in my life was closing, I knew that I had to prepare myself for the next step, high school. High school was going to be different and more challenging. In order for me to be successful, I was going to have to work harder because I understood that school was a challenge for me but I had conquered giants and made it through wilderness experiences, heck I was going to make it through high school. I was not going to let someone's opinion of me become my reality.

"I CAN DO ALL THINGS THROUGH CHRIST WHO STRENGTHENS ME."

PHILIPPIANS 4:13.

REFLECTIONS
"Building Your Ark"

What people surrounding you can be defined as "Ark Builders"?

_____
_____
_____
_____
_____
_____
_____
_____

Describe a time when you were a building block for someone else's Ark.

_____
_____
_____
_____
_____
_____
_____

5
TURNING WATER INTO WINE

Water into wine is symbolic of a transformation. This is not just an ordinary change but one that requires the movement of what may seem impossible. The challenges I faced prior to entering high school made me appreciate the ability to even be counted in the main stream of high school students. However, the time had come and I was ready. It was indeed time for me to go to high school.

At first high school was a struggle for me. I now believe it had more to do with the constant reminder of my disability than the actual disability itself. I always found myself trying to make excuses for the academic difficulty I was having simply because I did not want to be called the "Local Dummy". I do not think anyone would call me that to my face but I did not want to tempt fate. In addition, I hung out with many of the seniors because I already knew them thanks to Uncle Joe. So, my focus became working hard so that I could stay eligible to do the thing I loved the most, PLAY BASKETBALL!

It was so cool because everyone knew I was good because St. Mel was like a basketball Mecca in Chicago on the west side. If you went there and you were good everyone knew it. I will never forget three weeks before the season was about to start I was having trouble in my English class and I just couldn't get it, so I decided to get with two of my friends and cheat on a test.

Why did I even think about doing this? Well, simply put, I did not want to fail. Once I tried to cheat and of course I got caught because I had never cheated before and knew nothing about its dynamics. I had never been in trouble for cheating and this would be my first encounter with the Warden/Principal Paul J. Adams. Principal Adams ran a strict zero tolerance policy when it came to how students at his school were to behave. I was sitting in the office waiting to see him and I was terrified.

Knowing that I was related to Joe Jackson, he expected so much more out of me. That day, I sat in the office of what was known among my peers as "The Office of The Big Bad Wolf" and instead of chewing me up, he spoke life into me. I also believe that the life lesson my Mom instilled in me on facing your consequences was another saving factor for me that day. Because I did not lie, I took responsibility in my wrong and I asked for forgiveness Principal Adams had a different level of respect for me.

In his office, looking dead into my eyes, he decreed and declared right then that I would never get into trouble again. I knew then that he was planting a seed of prosperity in my life as that encounter changed my way of thinking towards my journey at St. Mel and Principal Adams. It was then that he had me to memorize and take to heart the mission statement of the school.

At Providence St. Mel, We Believe.
"We Believe in the creation of inspired lives
produced by the miracles of hard work.
We are not frightened by the challenges of reality,
but believe that we can change our conception of the

world and our place within it.

So, we work, plan, build and dream in that order.

We believe that one must earn the right to dream.

Our talent, discipline and integrity will be our

contribution to a new world. Because we believe that

we can take this place, this time, and this people, and

make a better place, a better time and a better

people. With God's help, we will either find a way or

make one"!

It was also on that day that he began a pattern that went on until I graduated. He told me about the greatness that was on the inside of me and how I just had to work hard if I wanted to pass and be successful. Every time he saw me, he would remind me of the greatness that was inside of me. That day, in the office of the Principal, a day that should have seen me being suspended was the day Mr. Adams challenged me to develop the character of a prosperous young man.

That conversation created a paradigm shift in my way of thinking. I wanted to work my way out of the

"LD" label not just for the offer of playing basketball, not to run away from the embarrassing things the other kids would say and think about me but so that I could be the best Simeon possible. I challenged myself to work harder, study more and ask for help when needed. Basketball practice was the reward to myself for the hard work I put in academically. I noticed even a rise in my game play.

The week of the Pep rally, I was pumped! The entire team waited for this day. Our coach was huge on team bonding. My friends, Puncho and Lamont, who I had already built court chemistry with, were on the team. The Pep rally was crazy with excitement.

When the team burst out of the locker room and into the gym, the crowd exploded with a thunderous applause! Chills went through my whole body as I was living my dream, the dream of playing in this gym and wearing that purple and gold with pride! It was electric. Every time we made a shot or someone dunked the ball, our classmates went wild!

This day plays in my mind as if it happened yesterday as this was the day I solidified in my mind my value as a team player. My friend Bernard Hughes went up for a layup and missed. As I went up behind him to get the rebound, it was as if a shot of energy came over me and as I went up for the ball, instead of grabbing it and pulling down the rebound, I tip dunked it back through the rim. That drew the crowd into a crazed roar! That assist is talked about today. It was one of the best feelings I ever had in my life. People who never spoke to me before were coming over and hugging me, shaking my hand and hi fiving me as I left the gym. One of the prettiest girls in the freshman class even handed me her number. I had made an impression.

Too bad, I spent the rest of the season on the bench. Wondering how that happened? Talk about freak accidents.

It happened in Mr. Murnan's gym class. We were playing soccer and I being the perfectionist that I am, every play that I was involved in was going to count. Coming down the court, I had my eyes fixed on the ball as did William another basketball player. I believe we were both doing what we had trained for in basketball. Going hard! It was evident when we both, overlooking the fact that the other opponent existed, went to kick the ball at the same time and SMASH!!!!!!!! His shin hit my shin and all you heard was a crack as I did a forward flip and landed on my back. The class went silent as I lay in pain praying that nothing was broken. Mr. Murnan, seeing that something was, called my mom and the school called the ambulance.

My mom and grandfather got to the school before the ambulance. She was frantic and all I kept thinking about was the game we had the next day and my possibility in getting on the court. The X-ray showed that I had a broken fibula. As the doctor explained the break in my shin, I asked the question, "How long would it be before I could play?"

"It would be a while," was the response as he gave

my Mom instructions on caring for my broken bone. William, on the other hand, was big boned and needed only to soak for the night. He was suited and ready for game that I heard about from the hospital bed. So, for the entire season, I was a cheering, broken leg, spectator from the bench.

Being in a cast and not being able to play forced me to focus on my grades. I had respect and support from my fellow students and even though I only played at the Pep rally, I was looked at as one of the best players on the team. The reason this meant so much to me is that I had people that told me I was going to be the low man on the poll when I went to high school and that I would not make it. In the grand scheme of things, it was about much more than basketball for me. It was about surviving and not becoming a statistic and making my mom and dad proud of the young man they were raising.

While things were going good in the school, there was this little problem outside the school. You see although my school was very good and safe, it was getting to school and my neighborhood that was the problem. Going to school on the CTA Chicago Transit Authority (CTA) caused a problem because the kids and gangbangers from the Henry Horner projects on the Westside of Chicago would always try to rob us for our bus and lunch money or even steal our clothes.

I did not play that. I would fight every time someone tried to jump me or steal my stuff and it started getting bad. My mom would be furious at the fact I couldn't go to school or be in the neighborhood without being approached with the unnecessary violence saying she wasn't going to let the streets take her baby and she meant that.

Besimbolic Lesson: Be open to new!

January of 1988 my mother decided that she was going to take her children away from the madness of Chicago to save our lives. My mother sat us down and told my big brother and I that we were going to be moving to Streamwood IL. Jake and I looked at each other like "What?" "Mama, what is a Streamwood?"

My mother laughed and said, "a place where you won't have to look over your shoulder when you're going to school or walking to the store. Streamwood is a place where I don't have to worry about my kids getting shot, and a place where you can focus on your education and being somebody." I knew my mother was fed up with the city but I never thought she would leave. At first, I cried. I asked if I could live with my grandmother and grandfather, my uncles, anything but leaving.

You see all my friends and everything that I had known in my short fifteen years on earth was in Chicago. I was in the school of my dreams playing basketball, getting good grades, had a pretty girl friend. Why should I leave?

When we went to St. Mel to get my transfer Mr. Adams did not want to see me go. He told my mother I could stay with him if she wanted me to stay. It was very tempting. I told Mr. Adams and my mom that I thought God had a plan for my life and I knew I had to go even if I did not want to. Mr. Adams smiled at me and said,

"Simeon go out there and be the best at everything you do" and with that I was off to a new and exciting chapter in my life. I had no idea of how it would turn out, but I was as ready as I would ever be. Streamwood, here I come!

My last day at St. Mel, was very emotional. Everyone was saying their good byes. Some of my friends even cried. It was bitter sweet as I was sad to be leaving but, excited at the possibility of a new and fresh start. We packed the moving truck all day and we headed out on a Friday night. The hour-long drive seemed to take forever but once we hit Streamwood we all took it in in silence. Pulling into the parking lot of the Robin Woods complex we were moving into, the first things we shared with each other was that it was darker than our old neighborhood. My mama laughed and said, "Welcome to the suburbs kids".

The place was amazing! We had a living room, kitchen, dining room, basement, two bathrooms and three bedrooms as well as a small back yard and front yard. I thought my mom had hit the lottery because I just knew we could not afford this. Even the dog, "KeKe" was in love. In Chicago, we had to keep her chained to the porch all day but now she had the luxury of a yard to roam around in.

Well, the next morning my mom woke us up bright and early to get the house together. Mama told me to go walk the dog. I asked her where I was supposed to walk the dog. Remember when we arrived in the evening it was dark and I did not know anything around there. When my mom told me to walk the dog down by the lake at the end of the parking lot, I knew we had done like the Jefferson and moved on up! A lake in the complex! And this lake had geese! I'm from the city and I had never seen anything like that. Come on geese!! The only time I had ever saw a duck or goose was on a cartoon or in a book at school. When I walked KeKe about 50 of them joined us. Not knowing what to do, I ran. Keke was on her own.

I ran back to the house as fast as I could and ran

through the door screaming "Mama, Mama, Mama"! It's a brunch of ducks out there by the lake!" My mother laughed and asked, "Boy, where is the dog?" I looked around and told her, "I don't know". Mama laughed again. "Boy, you left the dog?" We had to go find the dog and to this day, the family joke is the story about me running from the geese.

That Monday, March 7, 1988, I started a new chapter in my life and I was eager and terrified at the same time. Not because I was afraid of the people but I was nervous about being accepted. We heard so many things about suburban life that made me concerned about being the black boy from Chicago but I just kept saying to myself that this was all for a better purpose.

The first thing that was different was the fact that a bus picked us up for school. I was used to catching public transportation but there was not any out here in the suburbs. When my brother Jacob and I got on the bus, there were three other black kids; Shaun Dale, Duran and Chris. We connected immediately. Before my brother and I, they were three of ten African American kids at the school.

The school was huge and there was a farm right across the street from it with cows and horses grazing. I was amazed at what I was seeing. As I walked into the front doors, of the school for the first time with my big brother, I felt like all eyes were on us. As if everyone was saying "Who are these new kids? Where did they come from? Are they in a gang?" You might laugh and think it is funny but it is exactly how I felt.

My first day was the hardest. Coming from a school where everyone knew me and accepted my "LD" label. In this new environment, I felt as if these students would find out about my disability and make it even harder for me. I was going to a special class for reading and I did not want the label of being dumb. Remember, I was labeled LD. This new school, where I did not know anyone, was a tough transition. I was up for the challenge. I would come to school every day thinking of ways to turn the water I had been presented with in life, into wine.

Besimbolic Lesson: _When opportunity presents itself, take it._

I was in gym class one afternoon, bored out of my mind, standing against the wall watching the guys shoot hoops and the girls in their usual teen gossip huddles. Out of nowhere, Billy, one of the guys on the basketball team walked over and asked me if I wanted to play. My eyes lit up like a Christmas tree because this was right in my wheel house. If I could not do anything else, I could play some basketball. He did not know what he asked me.

We started playing and I just went into a zone. I was passing the ball, stealing the ball and scoring, at will. It was as if no one else was in the gym but the guys on the floor playing. I was in a trance and I would not be denied or let my team lose. You would have thought it was a playoff game.

Before I knew it all the students had stopped what

they were doing and everyone was standing around the court watching us play an intense game that no one wanted to lose. When I say everyone, I mean everyone. Not only were the students watching but also, the gym teacher had gone to get the head varsity coach, Kerry Sund and some of the football coaches to come and see the new kid from Chicago play. It was intense!

I went from being the new kid from Chicago that no one really talked to, to the talk of the day. After we finished playing, the guys from the basketball team that were playing came up to me. Shaking hands with me, they asked if I were going to join the team that next season. I had made an impression on them.

Later, the coaches begin to interrogate me asking questions like, "What school did you come? How long have you been playing? Are you serious about playing here in Streamwood?" The answer to all their questions was YES! YES! Heck YES!

What they did not know was that this is what I lived

for, what I worked hard for and what kept me off the streets in Chicago. I was so serious about basketball it would hurt me if I could not play.

Then one of the football coaches, Coach Zappia, the head sophomore football coach approached me. He asked me if I ever played football saying that I looked very fast and had quick feet. I told him the only football I ever played was in the hood in the field that was half grass and half dirt. He laughed and told me he would like me to come to camp that summer. I told him good luck convincing my mom into letting me play.

My mom never wanted me to play football. She thought it was too rough a sport for her boys to play. I wanted to try my hand at football and considering the lessons I had learned about being honest with my Mom, I manned up and told her my desire to play. She was not going for it at first but she eventually came around and made me promise to be careful. It was with the most joy ever that I could inform Coach Zappia that I would be joining them at football camp.

It was at football camp that I met Mark Rivera. Mark showed me the ropes and took me everywhere he went. His mom and step dad always gave me rides to practice and back home and our mothers became good friends behind that. Mark was a year older than me so he got his driver's license that summer during football camp. Once he had his license, he would pick me up in his Mustang. We were so close until he taught me how to drive his stick shift Mustang. I thought that was extremely cool. We were turning out to be the best of friends.

One day Mark hurt his ankle in practice and guess who had to drive us home? Yes, me. Mark's Mom took me to get my driver's license in my sophomore year the day after I turned 16. So as everything was moving along, I had friends, was playing sports and my grades were awesome but I missed my dad. I missed my friends in the city.

My Mom knew it so, she started letting me catch the

Metra with my friend Ardell, who was also from the city.
I would go back to the city to visit my Dad every chance
I got. During this time, my dad worked downtown at one
of the top hair salons as a hair stylist. Every time I saw
him he would ask me if I had any paper and before I
could answer he would go into his pocket and give me no
less than twenty dollars.

One time when Ardell and I were in Chicago, I saw
my dad and he wasn't quite himself. Wearing his army
fatigues and his half braided afro, a look my Dad would
never sport, he hugged me asking me something that
confirmed he was not fully himself. "Simmy, do have
any paper?" This was normal for him to inquire if I had
money as with that question he always pulled out money
for me. This time for some reason I answered, "Yes" and
he extended his hand and asked me if I could spot him
ten dollars to get himself something to eat. My dad never
asked me for money so feeling that he truly needed it I
gave it to him.

Before walking away from me he told me that he

missed me and my brothers, Jake and Dan. I told him I'd see him later and hurried off with Ardell. I did not discuss my dad for the rest of the day and Ardell respected my wish. I was not sure how I felt about seeing him like that but I knew that things were not right. On the bus heading back to Union Station, I saw my dad sitting on the bench at the bus stop on the corner of Roosevelt Road and Halsted looking bewildered as he slowly bit down on a sandwich. Ardell noticed him and tapped my shoulder saying, "Sim there go your pops"! I saw him and I ducked down on the bus so he could not see me.

My dad embarrassed me for the first time in my life. I did not know what was going on with him and I did not want to see him that way, so I hid until we got out of sight. Looking out the back of the bus, I watched him as he sat on the bench with what looked like the weight of the world on his shoulder. This wasn't the cool polished man that I knew. This looked like someone who was desperately in need of help. The messed-up part of it was that I wasn't there for my dad when he needed someone. I wasn't there to tell him come on dad let's go home. I did not help my dad because I was embarrassed by his appearance.

That was the last time I saw my dad alive. A few months later, my dad was murdered. The guilt I carried around after he died was monstrous and I was too ashamed to tell anybody what I was going through. Losing my dad at the age of sixteen, twelve days after my birthday devastated me but I decided that I was going to honor my dad by being successful. Therefore, I took all the anger, hurt, sorrow, disappointment and pain and I bottled it up, stored it on the inside of me and I moved full steam ahead.

Football was my tranquilizer. I played in a football game the next day after my father had died and no one could understand why I did it. They did not know how close we had gotten and how important our relationship was to me. My dad supported everything I did and always encouraged me to do and be better no matter what. People did not understand that my dad would have wanted me to play that game and be there for my teammates. They did not understand the odds that I beat to be in the position I was in. They did not understand that I was playing that game for my dad who I loved with all my being.

After the game was over, I went home and some of my family members were there, I packed up my clothes for the week and we went to the city to prepare for my dad's funeral. I did not know what to say or do; I just knew I was numb. I wasn't hungry and I wasn't talking to anyone. I needed some time to myself while trying to process this moment in my life so I called my God father and 8th grade teacher Mr. Harold Campbell. Campbell asked my mom if I could stay with him and his wife Lovey while the funeral arrangements were being made. Mom, understanding my grief, agreed to it.

While at the Campbell's house I had a chance to reflect and think about my pops and what he meant to me. I could cry and release some of the hurt and pain I was feeling at the time. I think I cried for about 5 hours straight at one point but, I felt like I was being cleansed and I felt like a weight was being lifted off my shoulders.

Besimbolic Lesson: *Allow grief to run its course.*

My dad was my world and it was going to be difficult facing the reality that he was gone. I saw a child on a bike and remembered how he taught me to ride. He wasn't going to be around when I decided to get married but he taught me to have the highest respect for women. My children would not have a grandfather and I was losing my fashion coach. My dad always talked about seeing me play in the Pros. He wasn't going to be around for that. This feeling was more overwhelming than when he moved out as a child because this time, he wasn't coming back. There would be no sneak visits to Grandma Henderson to see him. I allowed myself time to cry. I needed to cry.

The funeral was on a Saturday morning, the same day as a game. After the services, my cousin Reggie asked me what we were going to do. All I could think of was football. I wanted to make my Dad proud by playing in that game. So, I got in the car with my big brother Jake and a few of my cousins and we took a ride back out to Streamwood. I suited up and played in a football game five hours after burying my dad.

I knew my dad was with me for that game when I scored a touchdown. All I could think to do while at the goal, was look up to the sky and point the ball towards heaven letting my dad know that I scored that one for him. I knew he saw it and was well pleased with my effort and the fact that I did not give up. I went on to have a successful high school experience as a student and an athlete. I excelled in my grades and by my junior year was taken out of the LD classes.

I went on to become an all-conference football and basketball player. I was one of the first Black Homecoming Kings in my school's history and I always stayed eligible maintaining a "C" or "B" grade point average. Voted most popular and more importantly than anything else, graduating on time helped me realize that anything is truly possible. Being recruited by several schools for football and basketball as I finished as one of the top basketball and football players in the State of Illinois, made my mother very proud.

I never saw myself graduating from college and getting a degree but, thanks to my mother, my grandparents, uncles, teachers like Mr. Campbell, Coach Lil O and Big O, Mrs. O, Ms. Farley, Ms. Wearver, Mr. Miller, Mrs. Auto, Mr. Cole and I can't forget my big cousin Melvin Gunn, I defeated odds. I survived the wilderness, slayed giants, walked on water, faced my consequences and turned what seemed like water to wine while on my way to doing all the things people said I couldn't do.

My goal became to do things I never imagined I would and to get passed the image that being labeled placed me. I was not going to become a prisoner to the fear of succeeding simply because of where I came from and what I had gone through.

"TO GOD AND GOD
ALONE
BE THE GLORY!"
AMEN!

REFLECTIONS
"Turning Water into Wine"

What does it mean to turn "water into wine"?

_____
_____
_____
_____
_____
_____
_____
_____

What is the importance of the analogy "water to wine"?

_____
_____
_____
_____
_____
_____
_____
_____

PHOTO GALLERY

PHOTO GALLERY

Me at 15, with my mom

Me and Jake Suits made by mom

Me and Jake

MOM

PHOTO GALLERY

My First Trophy

FOOTBALL DAYS

PHOTO GALLERY

Me, Dad, Jake, Mom and Danyel

PHOTO GALLERY

Me and the Siblings
my brothers, Danyel and Jake, and my sister Charra

Me with my brothers

High school graduation

PHOTO GALLERY

COLLEGE GRADUATION

Dear Son:

I have seen God's hand in your life. Helping you through thick & thin. Your performance was only the work of God's helping hand. I thank God for a job well done in you! always put God first and he'll do the rest for you! Well done my son. Well done!

Love Mom
♡
always

A Job well done

Jim

ONE OF THE LAST LETTERS MY MOTHER WROTE ME.

ABOUT THE AUTHOR

From growing up on the west side of Chicago in one of its toughest neighborhoods, and being labeled learning disabled, to becoming a motivational speaker, an on-air TV personality for WCIU Chicago, as well as starring and co-starring in feature films and major TV series, Simeon has dedication his life to helping others walk in their purpose by using his life experiences.

Through the Eyes of a Man.

Made in the USA
Middletown, DE
30 January 2017